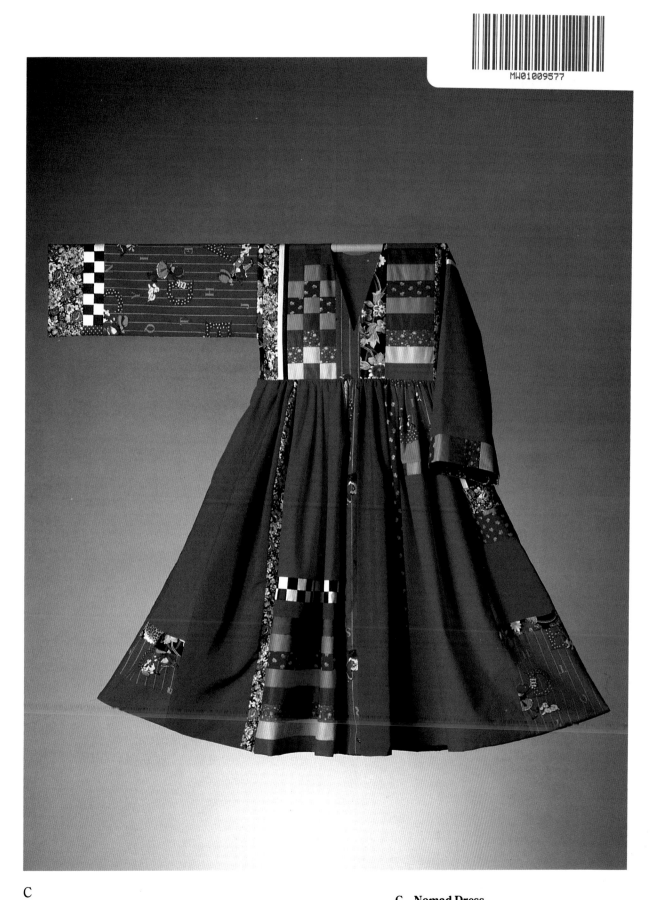

C

C. Nomad Dress
Strips of fabric machine pieced.

Pattern on page 20.

Patchwork Pants Top

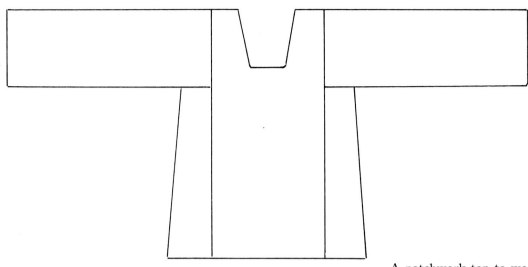

A patchwork top to wear with pants features three pattern pieces. A center panel extends from the front hem over the shoulder to the back hem, side panels are slightly shaped and sleeves are rectangles.

See color plate on page 6.

This pattern was adapted from an original folk costume from Palestine. The Palestine dress sewn in handwoven blue cloth is embroidered in silk with cross stitch.

TO DETERMINE FABRIC NEEDED: measure from lower edge of front hem over shoulder to back lower edge of hem. Hip line is recommended length for pants top. That measurement (52″ for a size medium)* of 45″ wide fabric is adequate for a pants top. If doing patchwork allow extra for piecing fabrics.

TO DETERMINE SIZE: take bust measurement and add two inches for ease (36″ + 2″ = 38″).* Determine width for center panel by holding tape measure across front of body inside shoulder line to see where sleeve line will be. This center panel width positions the sleeve seam at shoulder. Average width for center panel is 13″ to 14″. Take measurement of front and back panels (12″ for medium) (12″ + 12″ = 24″) subtract from adjusted bust measurement (38″ – 24″ = 14″). Divide the answer in half (14″ ÷ 2 = 7″) gives the width of side panels at top. Width of side panel at bottom is hip measurement plus 3″ for extra ease. Subtract width of center panel, divide answer in half for width of side panel at bottom (9″). Length of side panel is determined by width of sleeves. With garment folded at shoulder line sleeve width subtracted from center panel length equals length of side panel.

The sleeve is a rectangle. For width measure from armpit to armpit over shoulder add 2″ for ease (16″). The length of the sleeve is measured from the middle of back neck to wrist, subtract half the width of center panel (6″) for length of sleeve (22″).

WHEN CUTTING OUT GARMENT ALLOW SEAM ALLOWANCE ON ALL PIECES AND 2″ HEM.

*( ) denotes measurements for size medium

PIECED CLOTHING

Patterns for simple clothing construction
Yvonne Porcella

ISBN 0-914881088-4

Library of Congress Catalog Card Number 86-90565

First Printing 1980
Revised Edition 1987

Photographs by Elaine F. Keenan, San Francisco.
Printed in Hong Kong by Regent Publishing Services.
Revised Edition supervised by Roderick Kiracofe, San Franciso.

FRONT COVER: *Black, White and Red All Over* Haori pattern is pieced
appliquéd and hand quilted.
BACK COVER: Author and life-sized doll wearing pieced clothing. *Magic
Melody* outfit on left is Quilted Vest pattern done in string patchwork. *The
Jester* on right wears an adaptation of Patchwork Pants Top pattern in string
patchwork.

For information regarding workshops and lectures contact:
    Porcella Studios
    3619 Shoemake Avenue
    Modesto, California 95358
    209/524-1134

Yvonne Porcella's books are available from:
    C&T Publishing
    5021 Blum Road #1
    Martinez, CA 94553
    800/284-1114

ACKNOWLEDGMENTS

*My thanks to all my friends and my family who helped me in this
effort. And thank you to the many anonymous ancestors who
sewed the lovely folk costumes I am proud to own and enjoy.*

GUIDELINES TO FOLLOW WHILE USING THIS BOOK:

Cut garment shapes with a carpenter's square, which is a right-angle ruler measuring 16″ by 24″ available at hardware stores.

Prewash fabrics before cutting. Cotton, cotton blends, silk fabrics are recommended for use in pieced clothing. Generally do not mix silk and cotton fabrics in same garment.

Cut binding for seams on straight grain 1½″ wide. A straight-grain binding is suitable for all seams except those that curve. Use bias binding for curved seams. Sew binding with garment seams then hem raw edge of binding and slip-stitch edge to inside of garment.

Follow directions for individual pattern measurements to develop personal fit found in Patchwork Pants Top, Quilted Jacket and Pullover Shirt patterns.

A thin batt is recommended for use in quilted clothing. Cut batt same size as fabric pattern piece. Pin fabric, batt and lining together and hand quilt. Trim off batt that is forced outside the seam line by the quilting stitches before sewing seams. Use 1/4″ seam allowance for quilted clothes with batt. Sew seams with binding over seam, then hand-hem binding to inside of garment.

Some of the clothes featured in this book are pieced and then quilted to the lining only. There is no filler or batt between the two layers. This offers the look of a hand-quilted garment without the fullness of three-layer construction.

LIST OF PATTERNS

INTRODUCTION

For the past 20 years there have been changes in the manner of dress. We have experienced the popularity of denim and the progression of the casual comfortable look in clothing. Along with this we have come of age in the art of hand-crafted clothing, even going so far as to call it art. It is no longer embarrassing to say "I made it myself." Rather it is with pride that people are able to claim the fame they richly deserve for making clothing for themselves. These same people are able to experiment and make their own statement in how they dress.

I have been making my own clothing for many years and have developed an interest in simplifying the chore of selecting pattern and fabric, making room to cut it all out, and finally finding the time to actually sew. During the past few years I have done research in the field of folk clothing in an attempt to discover new ideas for clothing embellishment and fabric design. My research led to a discovery of not only fabric design but also of clothing construction. I learned that folk costumes were good examples of the efficient use of cloth. This stems from the fact that the cloth was precious, often hand-woven and sometimes of a very narrow width. Many cultures had very few clothes to wear so each garment had to be comfortable, useful and long-lasting. Many clothes served one owner for most of his or her life and often were patched, pieced and embellished to further the wearability of the garment. The basic shape of most folk clothing is in itself very simple so as not to waste fabric. Most garments are cut from rectangles of cloth and when laid flat represent a T-shape construction.

My study of folk clothing led to experimenting with the patterns themselves and from that experience comes this book. My first effort in pattern books was called *Five Ethnic Patterns*, a small book containing the instructions on how to cut and sew patterns in the ethnic style. Then came my second book *Plus Five* which included patterns for outer garments to wear over the T-shaped garments developed in *Five*. Since then I have explored the simplicity of this form of clothing construction and have begun to develop clothing made from simple pattern shapes using piecing and patchwork techniques. These patterns seem to lend themselves to quilting techniques since every pattern piece is cut from a flat shape and can be pieced or hand-quilted before assembling the garment. In an attempt to simplify clothing construction I have tried to keep the pattern instructions brief. The pattern pieces can be cut directly from the fabric since every shape is rectangular or cut from a rectangle. **No paper pattern** is necessary in this type of clothing construction. Just remember that in folk costumes a commercial pattern was not available and these people managed to clothe themselves for centuries.

The sample garments featured in the color section of this book are made from the patterns included and each article of clothing has been made in the patchwork style. Usually I piece the appropriate shape, line it, fill it with a batt if necessary, hand-quilt the piece and finally sew the pieces together with binding over the seams. I find this frees me from the rigidity of having to cut everything out at once. Also one can feel a tremendous sense of accomplishment if you set your goal to finish one unit of the garment at a time. It is rather like doing a sampler quilt in that each unit or rectangle or variation of a rectangle is finished and finally the garment assembled and the hand finishing done just like in a full-size quilt.

The biggest hurdle to overcome in using this book is to cut directly into the fabric without the aid of tissue-paper pattern pieces. I think you will enjoy the freedom of no-pattern sewing once you have tried this method.

A

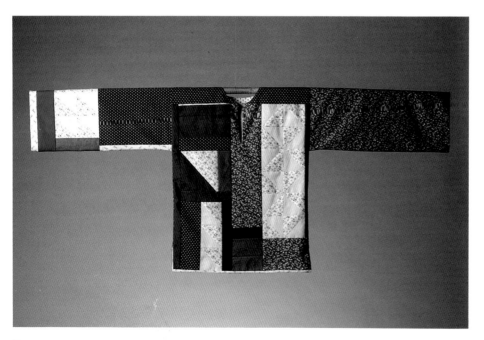

A. Patchwork Pants Top
Machine pieced, variations of Log Cabin.

Pattern on page 8.

B. Pullover Shirt
Strips of cotton with variations of pieced square.

Pattern on page 17.

B

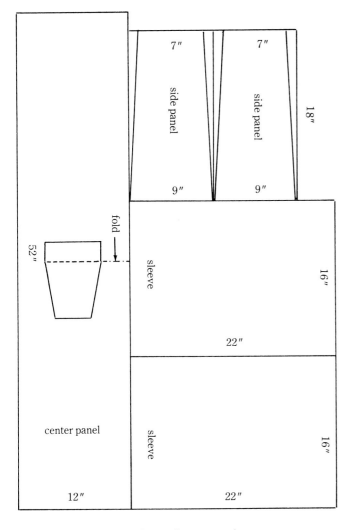

dimensions of pattern pieces

DIMENSIONS OF PATTERN PIECES will vary for each individual. Take measurements as directed and adjust for personal size. Make panels wider, narrower or longer after determining size. For medium size the center panel is 12″ wide by 52″ long or 26″ on fold plus 2″ for hem at both front and back edges. Sleeves are rectangles 16″ wide by 22″ long plus 2″ for hem at wrist. Side panels are 7″ wide at top and 9″ wide at bottom by 18″ long. Extra fabric is needed to face neck opening. Add seam allowance before cutting.

TO CUT OUT TOP use carpenter's square to mark center panel length and width on fabric with chalk pencil. Add seam allowance and hems before cutting. Match lower hem edges and fold center panel at shoulder line and mark horizontal center. Open out panel and mark vertical center. Face neck opening.

With right sides together place center of facing on top of center panel. Facing can be cut out of lightweight fabric and should be the width of the center panel, to catch in side seams, and about 18″ long. Mark neck opening on facing as desired. Use round neck opening template from the back of this book or as directed in suggested neck opening.

SUGGESTED NECK OPENING is a modified square opening. With ruler mark on facing with chalk pencil the shoulder horizontal line and intersect this line with a vertical line marking the center width. Draw neck opening as per diagram with opening measuring 6″ at back edge, 2″ at back side edges, 6″ down to front edge, 4″ across front. Sew on neck opening lines.

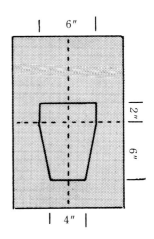

neck opening

neck facing

Cut out inside facing allowance leaving 5/8″ seam, slash corners, turn and press. Pin the neck facing along the center panel seam allowance to keep it in place.

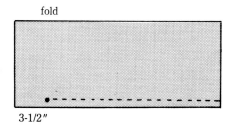

sleeve

SLEEVES are two rectangles plus seam allowance and hem. Cut out sleeves. Sew the sleeve seam from wrist to underarm stopping several inches before the edge. If your side panel measures 7″ at the top, stop sewing the underarm sleeve seam 3-1/2″ from edge. Include seam allowance in these measurements. Finish lower edge of sleeve with 2″ hem.

cutting layout
for side panel

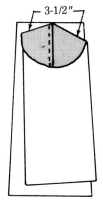

side panel
attaching sleeves

SIDE PANELS are cut from rectangles. Mark side panel width at top and width at bottom on rectangle. Draw line connecting top and bottom measurements and cut. When assembling final seams on garment be careful not to stretch side panel seams as they are slight bias cut and will be sewn to a straight edge panel.

Sew top of side panel to open edge of underarm sleeve seam. Open underarm seam and pin top of side panel in place, sew seam from both ends toward the middle.

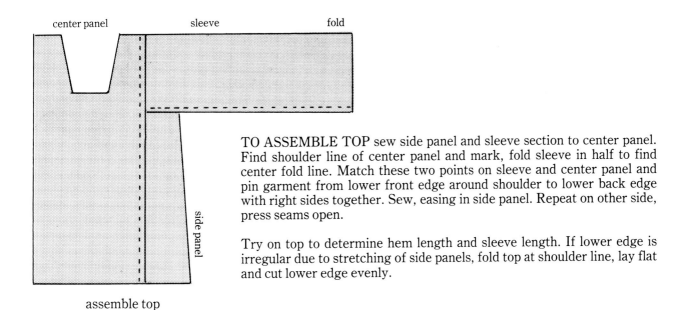

center panel   sleeve   fold

side panel

assemble top

TO ASSEMBLE TOP sew side panel and sleeve section to center panel. Find shoulder line of center panel and mark, fold sleeve in half to find center fold line. Match these two points on sleeve and center panel and pin garment from lower front edge around shoulder to lower back edge with right sides together. Sew, easing in side panel. Repeat on other side, press seams open.

Try on top to determine hem length and sleeve length. If lower edge is irregular due to stretching of side panels, fold top at shoulder line, lay flat and cut lower edge evenly.

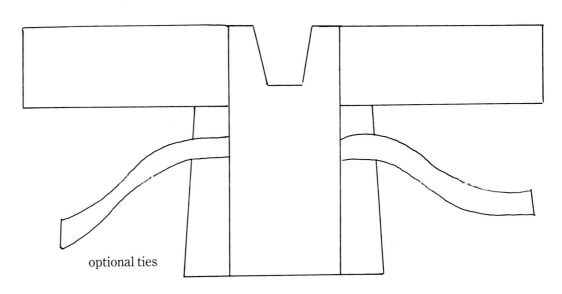

optional ties

Optional: add a tie 12″ down from shoulder line. Tie in back of top. Tie measures finished 2″ wide and 18″ long and is sewn into front panel seams.

Variations: round neck opening; neck opening with collar; shaped sleeves narrowing at wrist edge; sleeves gathered with cuff; longer length to wear as dress.

Quilted Jacket

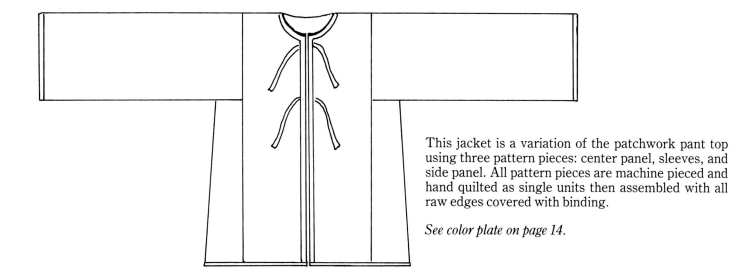

This jacket is a variation of the patchwork pant top using three pattern pieces: center panel, sleeves, and side panel. All pattern pieces are machine pieced and hand quilted as single units then assembled with all raw edges covered with binding.

See color plate on page 14.

TO DETERMINE FABRIC NEEDED: jacket will take a total of two yards of fabric for outside, two yards for lining and two yards of batting plus one yard for binding. If patchwork is used plan for enough yardage of each fabric so pieced fabric totals two yards. Use a thin batt or flannel for a comfortable jacket. Batt by the yard is not recommended.

TO DETERMINE SIZE: follow formula for determining size by measuring around bust with tape measure add two inches for garment ease (36″ + 2″ = 38″ for a dress)*. Add four inches ease for a jacket since it will be worn over another garment (36″ + 4″ = 40″). Hold tape measure across front of body to determine measurement for width of center panel. The tape should be positioned across upper chest from inside left shoulder to inside right shoulder. This will place sleeves at proper position. (For a dress this measurement for a medium size would be 12″, the center panel should be increased to 14″ width for a jacket.) For hip length jacket measure the center panel length from front hem line over shoulder to back hem line (52″ for medium).

The center panel provides both the front and back of the jacket (14″ front + 14″ back = 28″). Subtract the total front and back measurements from the adjusted bust measurement (40″ – 28″ = 12″).

Divide the answer in half (12″ ÷ 2 = 6″) gives the width of the side panels at top edge under the arm. For a jacket the total width at bottom is determined by taking hip measurement while seated and adding 4 inches (40″ + 4″ = 44″). Subtract width of center panel front and back (44″ – 28″ = 16″) divided by two equals the width of the side panels at bottom (8″ for medium, side panels measure 6″ at top and 8″ at bottom). Length of side panels is determined by width of sleeves. With garment folded at shoulder line sleeve width subtracted from center panel length equals length of side panel (17″).

The sleeve is a rectangle. For width measure from armpit to armpit over shoulder, add extra for ease (18″). The length of sleeve is measured from middle of back neck to wrist, subtract half the width of center panel (22″).

WHEN CUTTING OUT GARMENT ALLOW SEAM ALLOWANCE ON ALL PIECES.

*( ) denotes measurements for medium size

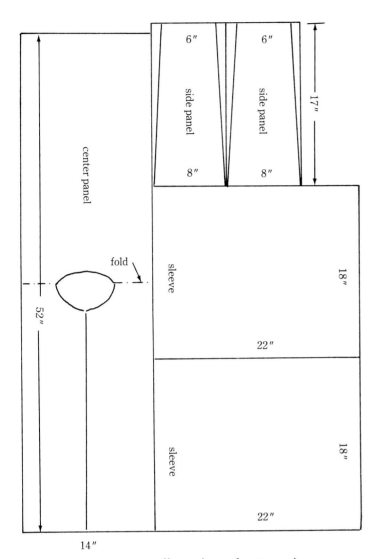

DIMENSIONS OF PATTERN PIECES will vary for each individual. Take measurements as directed and adjust for personal size. Enlarge pattern pieces or make them smaller. For medium size the center panel is 14″ wide by 52″ long or 26″ on fold. Sleeves are 18″ wide by 22″ long. Side panels width at top is 6″ and 8″ at bottom, length is 17″. Add seam allowance before cutting.

dimensions of pattern pieces

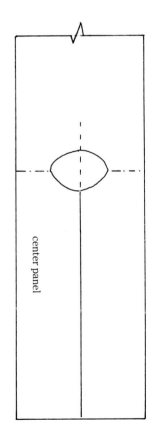

neck opening

TO CUT OUT JACKET use carpenter's square to mark center panel length and width on pieced fabric with chalk pencil. Add seam allowance before cutting. Use 1/4″ seam allowance. All seams will be finished with binding. Cut out center panel, batt and lining. Pin all three layers together. Match lower hem edges and fold center panel at shoulder line and mark center horizontal line. Open out panel and mark center vertical line.

NECK OPENING is round template found in back of this book. Mark on center panel and cut on cutting line. Slash front of jacket to hem along center vertical line. Stay stitch around neck opening using 1/2″ seam allowance. Do hand quilting as desired before finishing neck opening.

Jacket edges just meet in front, there is no overlap. Sample jacket has ties at neckline for closure. Make ties 10-1/2″ long from 1-1/2″ wide binding. Fold ties to 1/2″ width and top stitch. Pin ties to jacket front and finish raw edge of center front opening with binding sewing with 1/4″ seam. Slip stitch binding to inside.

Bind neck opening with bias binding.

Pattern continues on page 16.

D. Japanese Jacket
Narrow strips of cloth with pieced squares.

Pattern on page 31.

E. Quilted Jacket
Sleeves are antique fabric scrap of Grandmother's Flower Garden. Body of jacket machine pieced and hand quilted.

Pattern on page 12.

D

E

14

F

F. Haori

Black, White, and Red All Over, machine pieced, appliqued diamonds, hand quilted. Detachable sleeves.

Pattern on page 24.

Quilted Jacket continued.

SLEEVES are two rectangles cut including seam allowance. No hem is needed since sleeve is edged with binding. Cut lining and batt and do hand quilting as desired on sleeves. Finish wrist edge of sleeve with binding. Sew underarm seam from wrist stopping several inches before shoulder edge.

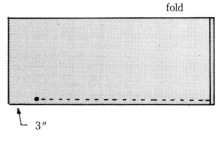

fold

3"

sleeve

LEAVE SEAM OPEN half the width of the top of the side panel. If side panel is 6" at top leave seam open 3". Include seam allowance in measurments.

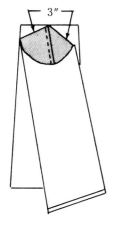

3"

SIDE PANELS are cut as shown in diagram. Line panel and fill with batt. Hand quilt as desired.

SEW TOP OF SIDE PANEL to unsewn edge of underarm sleeve seam. Open underarm seam flat and pin top of side panel in place. Stitch from each side of underarm seam to edge. If jacket is going to be reversible bind underarm seam.

side panel
attaching sleeve

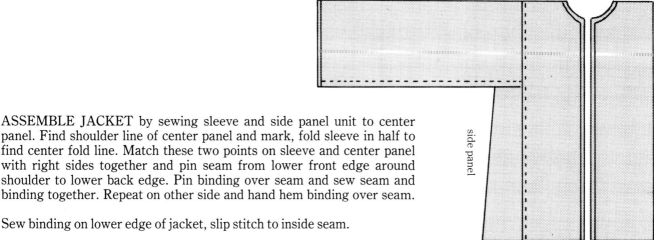

fold   sleeve   center panel

side panel

ASSEMBLE JACKET by sewing sleeve and side panel unit to center panel. Find shoulder line of center panel and mark, fold sleeve in half to find center fold line. Match these two points on sleeve and center panel with right sides together and pin seam from lower front edge around shoulder to lower back edge. Pin binding over seam and sew seam and binding together. Repeat on other side and hand hem binding over seam.

Sew binding on lower edge of jacket, slip stitch to inside seam.

assemble jacket

Pullover Shirt

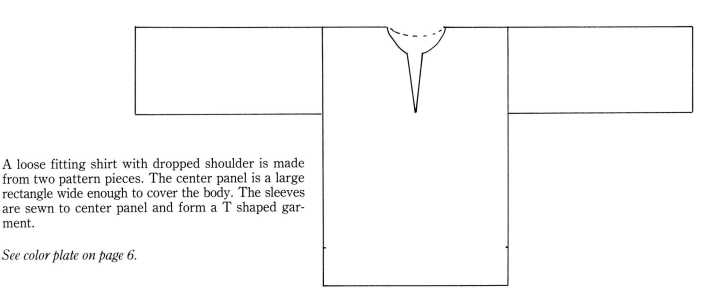

A loose fitting shirt with dropped shoulder is made from two pattern pieces. The center panel is a large rectangle wide enough to cover the body. The sleeves are sewn to center panel and form a T shaped garment.

See color plate on page 6.

The original shirt from South America can be worn by men or women depending on width of center panel. Shirt is pieced together with scraps of colorful handwoven cloth.

TO DETERMINE FABRIC NEEDED: measure from lower edge of front hem at hip level over shoulder to back lower edge of hem. That measurement plus hem allowance in 45″ wide fabric is adequate for pullover shirt. If doing patchwork allow extra fabric for piecing.

TO DETERMINE SIZE: for women take measurement of hips and add two inches for ease (38″ + 2″ = 40″)*. For men measure chest and add ease. Divide the answer in half for width of front and back panels (20″). Length of shirt is measured from desired lower edge over shoulder to back lower edge (54″ plus hem). Be sure to add seam allowance on all seams and two inches for front and back hem on center panel. Sleeve width is measured from armpit to armpit plus ease (18″). Length of sleeve is measured from middle of back neck to wrist, subtract half the width of center panel. Since this is a drop shoulder the sleeve will be shorter. To be sure of length of sleeve, try on center panel after neck opening has been made and measure length of sleeve from edge of center panel.

WHEN CUTTING OUT SHIRT ALLOW SEAM ALLOWANCE ON ALL PIECES.

*( ) denotes measurements for medium size

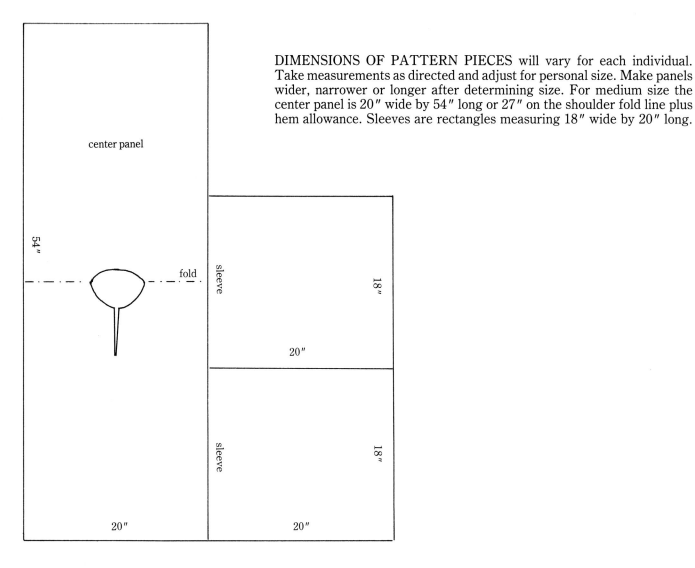

DIMENSIONS OF PATTERN PIECES will vary for each individual. Take measurements as directed and adjust for personal size. Make panels wider, narrower or longer after determining size. For medium size the center panel is 20″ wide by 54″ long or 27″ on the shoulder fold line plus hem allowance. Sleeves are rectangles measuring 18″ wide by 20″ long.

dimensions of pattern pieces

TO CUT OUT SHIRT use carpenter's square to mark width and length of center panel directly on fabric with chalk pencil and cut. Add seam allowances and hem before cutting. Fold center panel in half matching hem edges and mark center shoulder line.

For facing cut a separate piece of fabric of lighter weight material the same width of center panel (20″ plus seams on both edges) and about 18″ long. With right sides together place center of facing on horizontal shoulder line, mark neck opening on facing. Sample shirt has round neck opening from the template in the back of this book. Sew neck opening on sewing lines. Cut out center leaving 1/2″ seam allowance. Clip curve, turn facing to inside and press.

Cut out two sleeves plus seam allowance and hem. The sleeves can be made narrower and a gusset added under the arm for extra ease if desired.

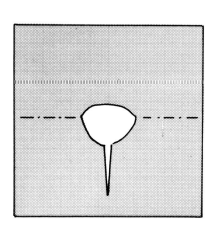

facing with neck opening

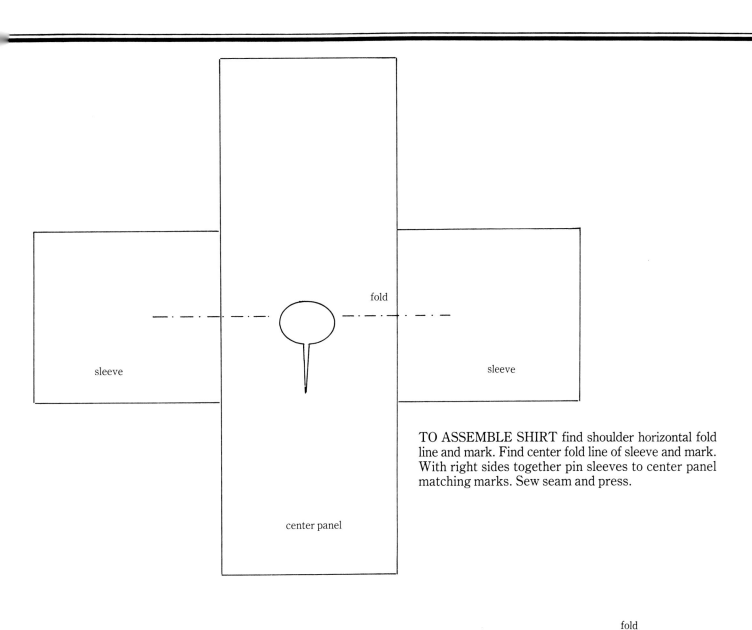

TO ASSEMBLE SHIRT find shoulder horizontal fold line and mark. Find center fold line of sleeve and mark. With right sides together pin sleeves to center panel matching marks. Sew seam and press.

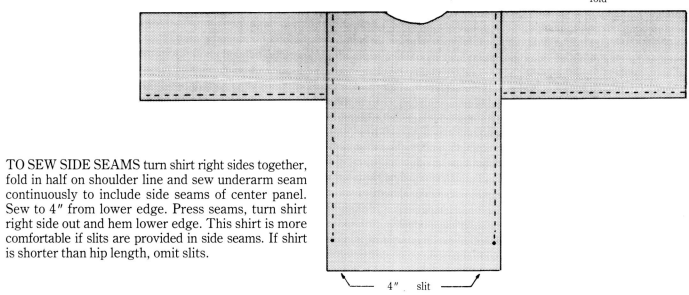

TO SEW SIDE SEAMS turn shirt right sides together, fold in half on shoulder line and sew underarm seam continuously to include side seams of center panel. Sew to 4″ from lower edge. Press seams, turn shirt right side out and hem lower edge. This shirt is more comfortable if slits are provided in side seams. If shirt is shorter than hip length, omit slits.

Nomad Dress

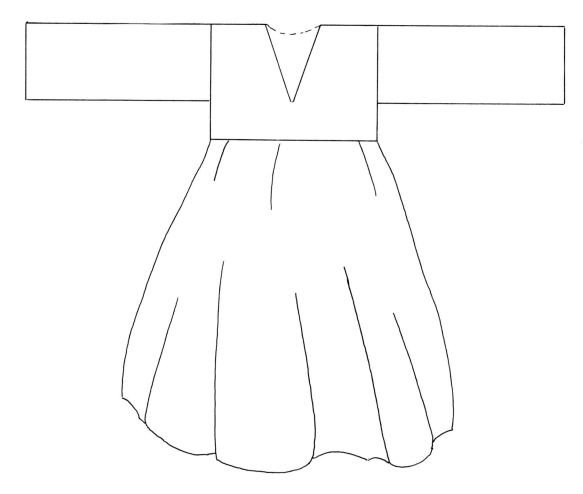

This dress pattern has a very full gathered skirt. The pattern can be made as drawn in dress length or shortened to a hip length top. The bodice has two pattern pieces; center panel shortened to a yoke and sleeves. This style fits the body loosely and slips over the head. Basic construction of yoke and sleeves is like pullover shirt. Add gathered skirt to front and back yoke.   *See color plate on page 7.*

The original dress is a Kuchi or nomad dress from Afghanistan. The dress is hand pieced with lavish embroidery on the bodice, sleeves and hem. The Kuchi dress is sewn in silk fabric and is hand quilted to a cotton lining.

TO DETERMINE FABRIC NEEDED AND DRESS SIZE: take bust measurement and add ease (36″ +2″ = ·38″)*. Yoke should be wide enough to slip over the head and bust. Add seam allowance before cutting. Divide the yoke measurement in half for front and back panels. Length of yoke is determined by where gathers begin—at bust line or below, measure over shoulder to back yoke edge (24″). Skirt fabric needed is determined by how long and full skirt will be for either a dress or top. A very full skirt has two yards of fabric gathered to front yoke and two yards of fabric gathered to back yoke. Approximately 5 yards of fabric is needed for dress.

Cut out yoke and sleeves with carpenter's square and make neck opening in yoke.

WHEN CUTTING OUT GARMENT ALLOW SEAM ALLOWANCE ON ALL PIECES.

*( ) denotes measurement for medium size

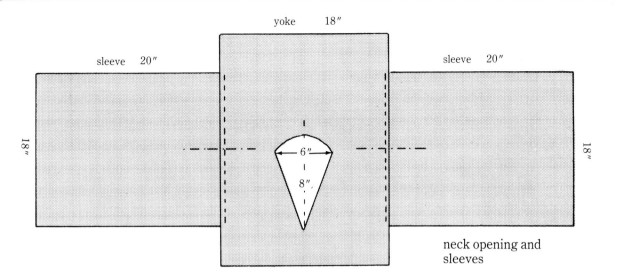

yoke 18"

sleeve 20"   sleeve 20"

18"   18"

6"

8"

neck opening and
sleeves

NECK OPENING AND SLEEVES: cut yoke desired size (18" wide by 24" long for medium size) plus seam allowance. Cut another yoke exactly the same size out of lightweight fabric for facing. With right sides together mark center horizontal line and vertical line on facing. Draw neck opening on facing and stitch on drawn line. Cut away center leaving 1/4" seam allowance. Clip curve, turn facing to inside and press.

Find measurements for sleeves as directed in pullover shirt. Cut out sleeves plus seam allowance and hem (18" by 20" for medium size). Find center horizontal fold on sleeves and match right sides together with center fold line on yoke. Sew sleeves to yoke.

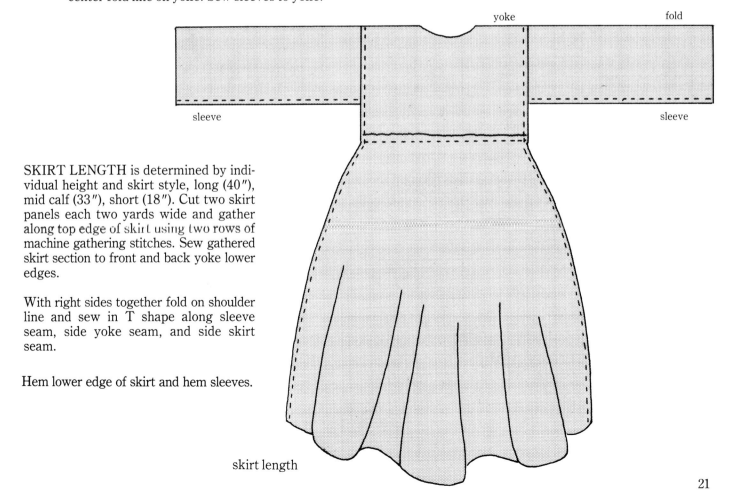

yoke   fold

sleeve   sleeve

SKIRT LENGTH is determined by individual height and skirt style, long (40"), mid calf (33"), short (18"). Cut two skirt panels each two yards wide and gather along top edge of skirt using two rows of machine gathering stitches. Sew gathered skirt section to front and back yoke lower edges.

With right sides together fold on shoulder line and sew in T shape along sleeve seam, side yoke seam, and side skirt seam.

Hem lower edge of skirt and hem sleeves.

skirt length

Quilted Vest

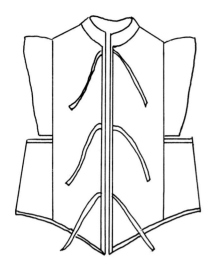

This short vest is reversible and quilted for added warmth. It follows the basic pattern shapes of the quilted jacket except this vest has a shaped shoulder seam. The vest consists of a center panel front and back and has side panels. The sleeves are omitted in favor of a shaped band at shoulder edge. The vest has a stand up collar and closes with ties. The lower edge is curved. *See color plate on page 46.*

TO DETERMINE FABRIC NEEDED: the sample vest is patchwork style with scraps of fabric used for piecing. Approximately one yard of 45" wide fabric is needed for vest plus the same amount for lining. The sample vest is pieced to an underlining in the string patchwork method. Batting can be used but should be thin for a comfortable vest. Each pattern shape is pieced and hand quilted before assembling the vest. All seams are finished with bias binding. Allow one yard contrasting fabric for binding.

TO DETERMINE VEST SIZE: use formula for quilted jacket pattern, bust plus ease, determine width of center panel and side panel measurements. Length of vest is 6" below waist in front and curves to 2-1/2" below waist at sides. Add 1/4" seam allowance.

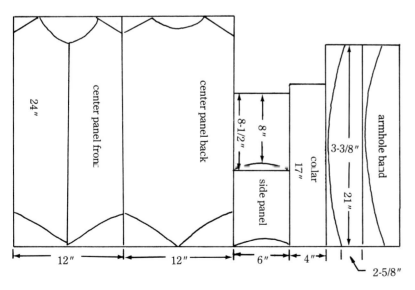

dimensions of pattern pieces

DIMENSIONS OF PATTERN PIECES: center panel has front and back panel (12" wide by 24" long)*. Shoulder edge is 1-1/2" angled off from neck opening. Use neck opening template found in back of book. When marking neck opening be sure to allow for 1/4" seam on shoulder which comes into neck opening. Shape lower edge of vest by curving 3-1/2" from center point to outer side. Armhole is 10-1/2" long. Side panel length is from curved edge of center panel up to edge of armhole (medium size side panel measures 8 1/2" long by 6" wide). Collar is rectangle 4" wide by 17-1/2" long. Collar is folded on fold line and interfaced. Armhole band is 4" wide by 21" long and curved to measure 2-5/8" at each end and 3-3/8" in center. Cut four bands and two interfacings.

WHEN CUTTING OUT GARMENT ALLOW 1/4" SEAM ALLOWANCE ON ALL PIECES.

*( ) denotes measurements for medium size

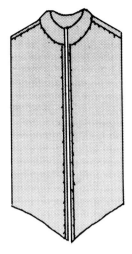

center panel

CUT OUT CENTER PANEL front and back and shape shoulders and bottom edge. Line center panel and cut out neck opening on back and front. Slash center front to lower edge. Bind center front edges with binding putting ties in seam if desired. Ties are 10-1/2" long and finished to 1/2" wide. Sew shoulder seams with binding over seam. Hand hem binding to lining.

collar

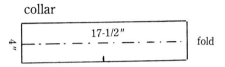

COLLAR is 17-1/2" long by 4" wide and will fit on template neck opening which can be found in back of this book. Stay stitch neck opening with 5/8" seam allowance and clip curve. Interface collar and sew collar with 5/8" seams to neck edge matching center of collar to center back neck, ease around curve. Fold collar on fold line right sides together and stitch across ends. Turn collar to outside and press. Hand hem collar inside to lining.

CUT SIDE PANELS AND ARMHOLE BANDS. Line side panels and hem top edge of side panel with bias binding. Armhole bands and lining are 21" long by 3-3/8" wide curving to 2-5/8" at ends. Interface and sew band and lining with 5/8" seam along curved edge and across ends with 1/4" seams. Clip the curve, turn band to outside and press. Top stitch band or hand quilt to stiffen.

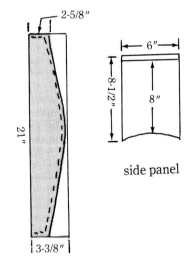

armhole band

side panel

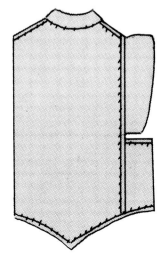

ASSEMBLE VEST by sewing armhole band and side panel to center panel with bias binding over seam. Hand hem binding to inside lining.

Finish lower curved edge of vest with bias binding.

Variation: vest can be made without armhole band and collar and with straight bottom edge.

Haori Coat

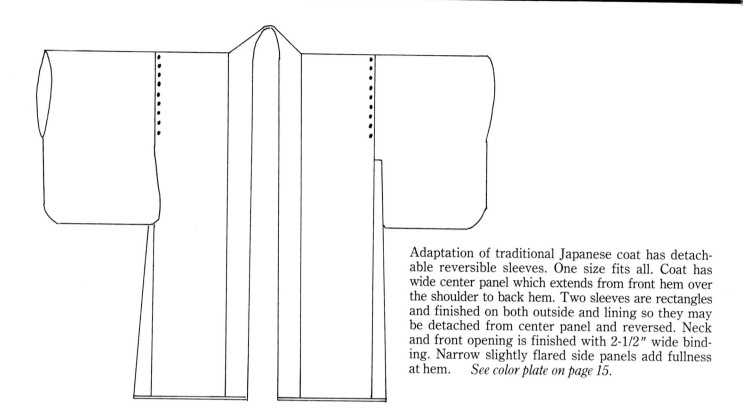

Adaptation of traditional Japanese coat has detachable reversible sleeves. One size fits all. Coat has wide center panel which extends from front hem over the shoulder to back hem. Two sleeves are rectangles and finished on both outside and lining so they may be detached from center panel and reversed. Neck and front opening is finished with 2-1/2" wide binding. Narrow slightly flared side panels add fullness at hem. *See color plate on page 15.*

The original Japanese coat is sewn in silk fabric with a contrasting lining. The long rectangle sleeves are lined and sewn to the coat so that the lower nine inches of the sleeve is not attached to the center panel. This allows for an opening under the arm and the sleeve can be used as a pocket or to hold sleeves of a kimono.

TO DETERMINE FABRIC NEEDED: one size fits all although coat center panel width and sleeve length can be adapted to larger or smaller sizes. Center panel is 24" wide and extends from front hem over shoulder to back hem, a total length of 72" or 36" in front and 36" in back. Sleeves are rectangles measuring 12" wide by 36" long or 18" on fold at shoulder. Neck binding is folded in half lengthwise so that 2-1/2" shows on front of coat and 2-1/2" on lining side. Length of neck binding is length of front center panel times two plus 8" across back of neck. Coat is completely lined. Allow same amount of fabric for outside of coat and lining, approximately 3 yards fabric for each side. Sleeves are detachable by means of tiny elastic loops and buttons. Purchase one yard elastic lingerie loops and buttons to match fabric.

WHEN CUTTING OUT GARMENT ALLOW SEAM ALLOWANCE ON ALL PIECES.

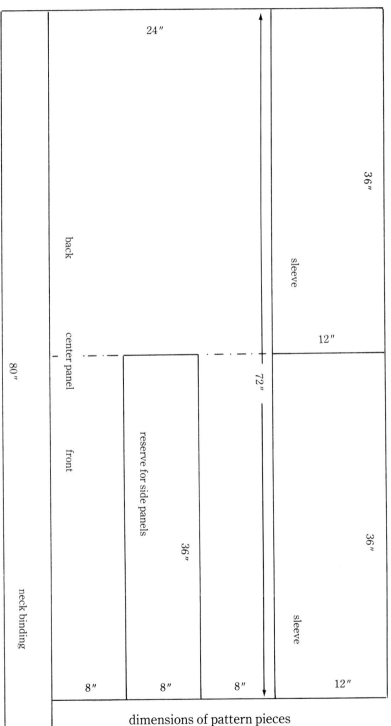

dimensions of pattern pieces

DIMENSIONS OF PATTERN PIECES: overall length of center panel is 72″ or 36″ on fold. The width is 24″. Cut two panels, one for outside and one for lining. Batting may be used for a heavier coat and as filler to show hand quilting stitches. Use very thin batt or flannel. Cut batt same size as fabric pieces.

Sleeves are 36″ long by 12″ wide.

Neck binding is 80″ long by 5″ wide. Add seam allowance on all pieces before cutting. If doing patchwork with batt allow 1/4″ seams. Allow 1/2″ seams for two layer coat.

Reserve 8″ by 36″ long panel cut from center front for use as side panels.

TO CUT OUT COAT begin with sleeves and if patchwork is used, piece fabric together in appropriate size for pattern pieces then proceed with coat construction. String patchwork is suggested for the sleeves. Cut two flannel or muslin fabric pieces 12″ by 36″ plus seams for underlining and sew fabric pieces to underlining. Cut separate lining.

Using carpenter's square mark the center panel width and length directly on fabric with chalk pencil. Cut out center panel with the lining pinning wrong sides together of outside fabric and lining. Handle as one piece of fabric.

Cut out neck binding plus seam allowance, interface neck binding.

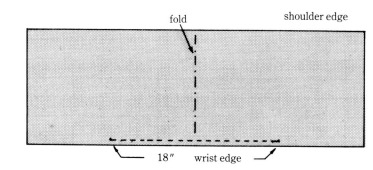

shoulder edge

elastic loops

fold

12″

36″ – wrist edge

sleeves with elastic loops

SLEEVES: cut two rectangles 12″ by 36″ from pieced fabric, plus seam allowance then cut two lining pieces. Sleeve will be finished with no raw edges then attached to coat by elastic loops and buttons. On shoulder edge of sleeve place 18″ long piece of elastic loop (called lingerie loop, elastic loops spaced one inch apart on narrow band) on seam allowance and zig zag in place. Loops should face away from shoulder edge.

fold   shoulder edge

sleeve and lining

18″   wrist edge

With right sides together sleeve and lining, sew along wrist edge of sleeve for 18″ in the center of sleeve, that is, sew 9″ either side of center fold.

fold

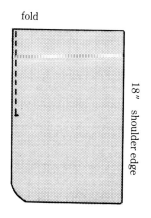

18″   shoulder edge

Fold sleeve and lining on fold line and mark lower corner of wrist edge 1″ from point of corner and cut gentle curve.

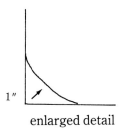

1″

cut curve on wrist edge

enlarged detail

sleeve   lining

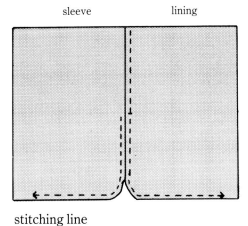

stitching line

WITH THE SLEEVE folded on center fold and right sides together, pull out lining from sewn wrist edge so lining and sleeve look like the drawing. Stitch lower edge of sleeve and lining beginning at last stitch of wrist edge seam and continuing across bottom edge. Repeat on lining. Leave shoulder edge open on both sleeve and lining.

fold

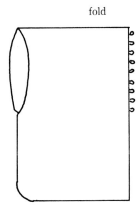

TURN SLEEVE to outside and tuck lining inside sleeve wrong sides to wrong sides. Press seam open and slip stitch by hand the raw edge of lining and sleeve shoulder edge so elastic loops extend outside the seam.

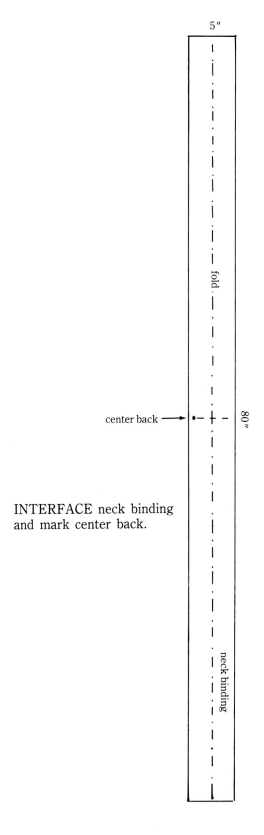

5″

fold

center back →

80″

neck binding

INTERFACE neck binding and mark center back.

27

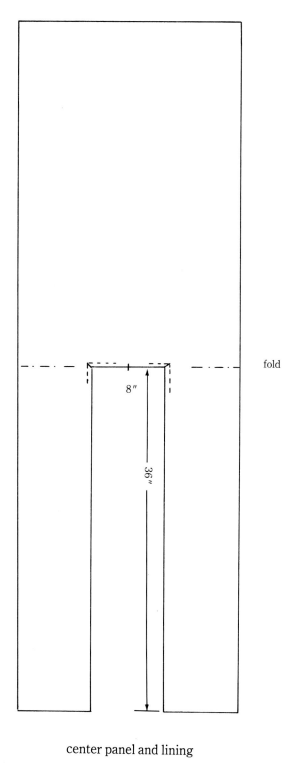

8″

36″

fold

center panel and lining

PIN CENTER PANEL and lining wrong sides together and cut out 8″ by 36″ panel from front for neck opening. This coat does not close in front when worn but hangs open about three inches.

Reserve the 8″ by 36″ piece cut from the center for use as side panels. Keep pinned wrong sides together.

Stay stitch at corners of neck opening along seam line and clip corners.

Mark center back of neck opening on center panel and match up with center back of neck binding and sew binding to coat right sides together.

Fold neck binding on fold line, turn in seam allowance and slip stitch binding along seam line to inside lining of coat.

stay stitch and clip
corners, mark center
back

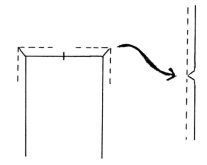

Clip in corners of neck opening will open out so straight edge can be sewn in one continuous seam.

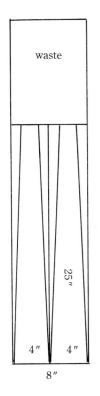

side panels

CUT TWO SIDE PANELS from the 8″ wide piece reserved from center front. This piece is still pinned wrong sides together and should be handled as one piece of fabric.

Side panel is 11″ shorter than the center panel and the sleeve is attached for only 9″. This leaves an opening under the arm of 2 inches.

Mark with chalk pencil on fabric 11″ from top of panel. Mark remaining 25″ in half lengthwise. From the two 4″ by 25″ panels, cut two side panels each measuring when finished 1″ at top and 3″ at bottom. Include seam allowance before you cut.

Now hem the top of the narrow side panel by sewing wrong sides together, turn and press.

FOR JOINING COAT separate center panel outside fabric from lining. Sew two layers of side panel (outside and lining) to outside of coat right sides together of side panel and coat. Begin at lower edge of center panel front, stitch to top of side panel. Begin again at lower edge of center panel back, stitch to top of side panel. Be careful not to sew lining in this seam.

Slip stitch lining to inside side seams. Continue to slip stitch along armhole seam allowance to hem lining to coat along armhole edge.

slip stitch lining to side panel seam, continue along armhole edge of coat

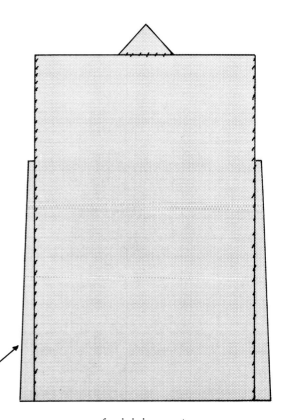

for joining coat

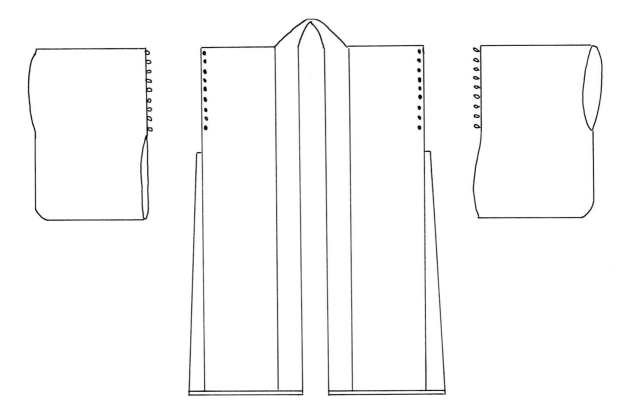

FINISH COAT by sewing binding to lower edge and hand hem to inside. Cut 1-1/2″ wide straight grain binding long enough to hem raw edge of bottom including neck band.

Sew buttons on armhole edge of coat.

Alternatives: if elastic loops are not available, try narrow ties or snaps or separating zipper.

If you prefer to sew sleeve to coat and not attach with buttons, follow instructions for sleeves found in Japanese jacket pattern.

Neck band can be folded back at neck for alternative style front opening.

Japanese Jacket

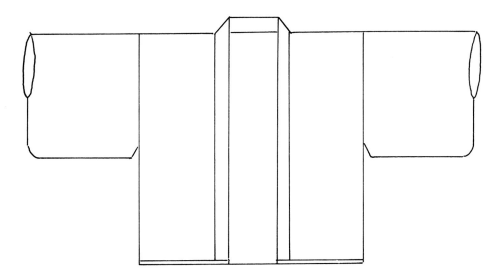

Short jacket has a center panel which extends from front lower edge over shoulder to back lower edge. Kimono style sleeves have an opening under the arm. Narrow neck binding edges the front. Jacket does not meet in front but hangs open.

Original jacket is in silk and lined with silk. This version can be made in patchwork style using cotton or silk fabrics. Jacket is lined.

TO DETERMINE FABRIC NEEDED: one size fits all although jacket center panel width can be adapted to larger or smaller sizes. Center panel is 24″ wide and extends from front hem over shoulder to back hem, a total length of 48″ or 24″ in front and 24″ in back. Sleeves are almost square measuring 12″ wide by 13″ long on the fold line at the shoulder. There is an opening under the arm. Neck band is 1-1/2″ wide on the fold and long enough to go around front opening. Allow 1-1/2 yards of fabric for outside and the same for lining.

Sample jacket is featured in patchwork. Narrow pieces of cotton fabric were cut and seamed together to form each pattern piece.
See color plate on page 14.

WHEN CUTTING OUT GARMENT ALLOW SEAM ALLOWANCE ON ALL PIECES.

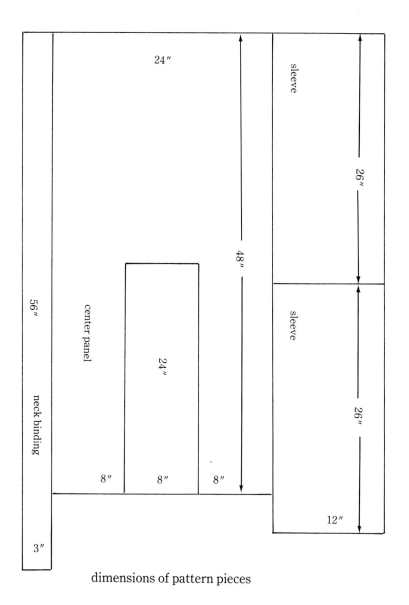

dimensions of pattern pieces

DIMENSIONS OF PATTERN PIECES: overall length of center panel is 48″. Allow extra for hem or a narrow binding can be used as finishing for hem. Width of center panel is 24″. Sleeves are 12″ wide by 26″ long or 13″ long from the shoulder fold line. Cut lining the same size as pattern pieces. Add seam allowance to pieces before cutting. Neck binding is 56″ long by 3″ wide plus seams. Interface neck binding.

FOR CUTTING OUT GARMENT use a carpenter's square to measure pieces accurately. Draw with chalk pencil directly on fabric and cut. If doing patchwork, piece fabrics first then cut out garment.

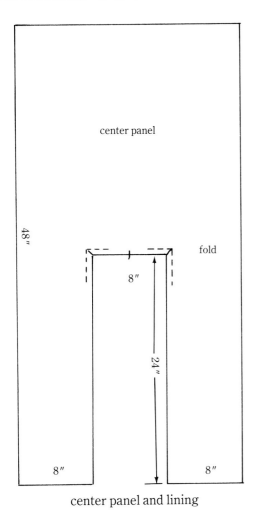

center panel and lining

CENTER PANEL is cut with outside fabric and lining pinned wrong sides together and treated as one fabric. Mark shoulder fold line which is half the length of center panel. Cut out 8″ wide by 24″ long panel from center front for neck opening.

Mark center back on neck opening.

Stay stitch at corners of neck opening on seam line and clip corners. Clip will open out so straight edge binding can be sewn in one continuous seam.

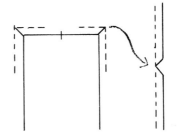

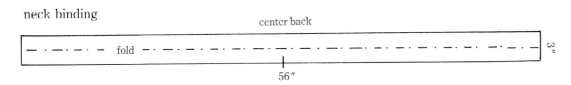

CUT OUT NECK BINDING 3″ wide by 56″ long plus seam allowance. Interface binding and mark center back.

Match center back of neck opening with center back of neck binding and with right sides together stitch neck binding to jacket.

Fold neck binding on fold line, turn in seam allowance on edge and slip stitch binding along seam line to inside lining.

CUT OUT TWO SLEEVES and lining. Patch fabric for outside sleeve if desired. Sleeve measures 12″ wide by 26″ long. Add seam allowance.

sleeve and lining

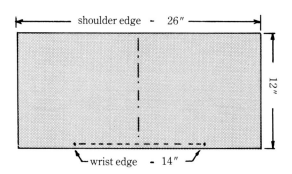

With right sides together put sleeve fabric and lining together. Mark center fold line. Seam along wrist edge for 14″ starting at fold line and stitching 7″ on either side of fold.

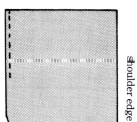

Fold sleeve and lining on fold line and mark lower corner of wrist edge 1″ from point of corner and cut gentle curve.

cut curve on wrist edge

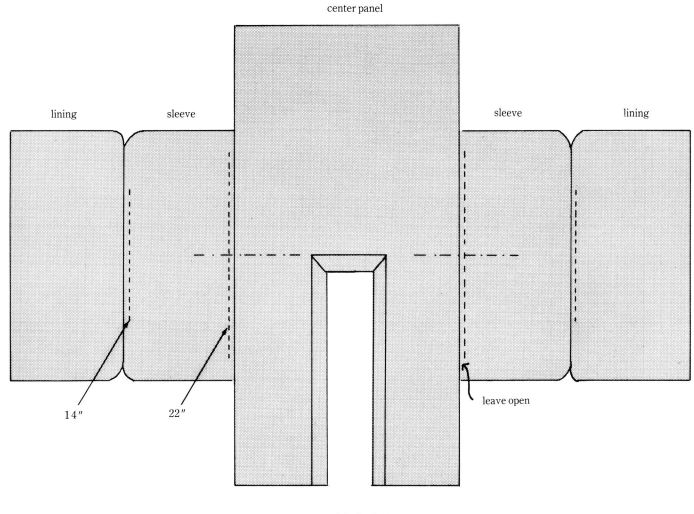

center panel

lining   sleeve   sleeve   lining

14″

22″

leave open

assemble jacket

TO ASSEMBLE JACKET sew sleeve to center panel. Separate outside fabric and lining of center panel. Mark center fold line on center panel. Match with fold line of sleeve. With right sides together sew sleeve to jacket being careful not to sew lining in this seam. Sew sleeve to jacket for 22″ or 11″ from either side of fold line leaving last 2″ of seam open.

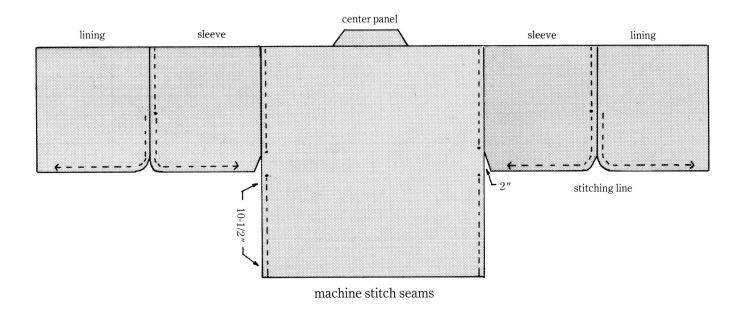

lining sleeve center panel sleeve lining

10-1/2″

2″

stitching line

machine stitch seams

TO SEW SEAMS fold jacket on fold line with right sides together and stitch side seams. Then stitch lower edge of sleeve and lining as drawn.

Jacket side seam is sewn for 10-1/2″ from lower edge leaving 2″ opening in side seam underarm.

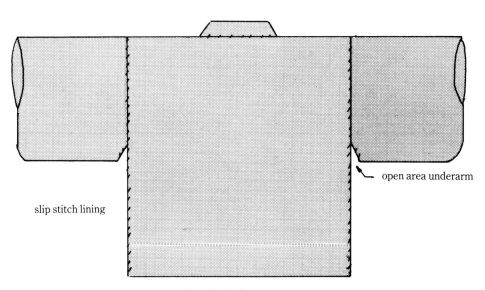

open area underarm

slip stitch lining

hand stitch seams

TURN BACK LINING of sleeve wrong sides together over sleeve and slip stitch lining of sleeve with jacket lining along sleeve seam. Then stitch jacket lining side seams.

Finish the opening under the arm by slip stitching lining to jacket side seam. Repeat slip stitching on sleeve edge.

Hem lower edge of jacket or bind with binding.

Tibetan Sleeveless Coat

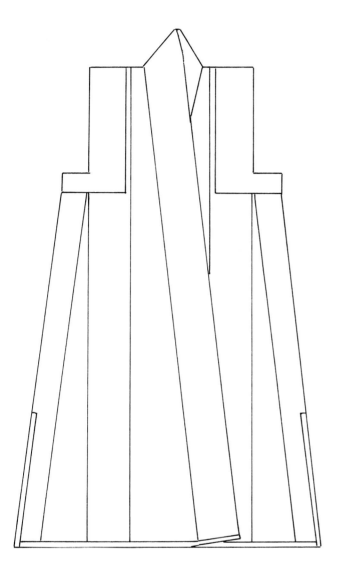

This is a long sleeveless coat that has narrow panels alternating with long triangular panels. The center panel is wide and forms an exaggerated lifted shoulder which is trimmed with a decorative fabric. The coat is loose fitting, reversible and all seams are covered with binding. The neck band is wide and folds down arond the neck. The front panel can overlap or hang open. *See color plate on page 55.*

The original coat from Tibet is sewn in wool felt and has gold brocade trim on the shoulders.

TO DETERMINE FABRIC NEEDED: the sample coat was sewn in string patchwork technique. All pieces were stitched to an underlining. Three and 1/2 yards of 45″ wide fabric was used for underlining. Three yards of fabric were purchased for the long narrow panels and neck band. Half yard lengths of various fabrics were purchased and cut in strips for the patchwork. The same amount of lining is necessary as for outside of coat. All seams are finished with 1-1/2″ wide straight grain binding sewn with 1/4″ seam allowance. Purchase one yard for binding.

This coat is very loose fitting and one size fits all. If desired cut panels narrower for smaller size.

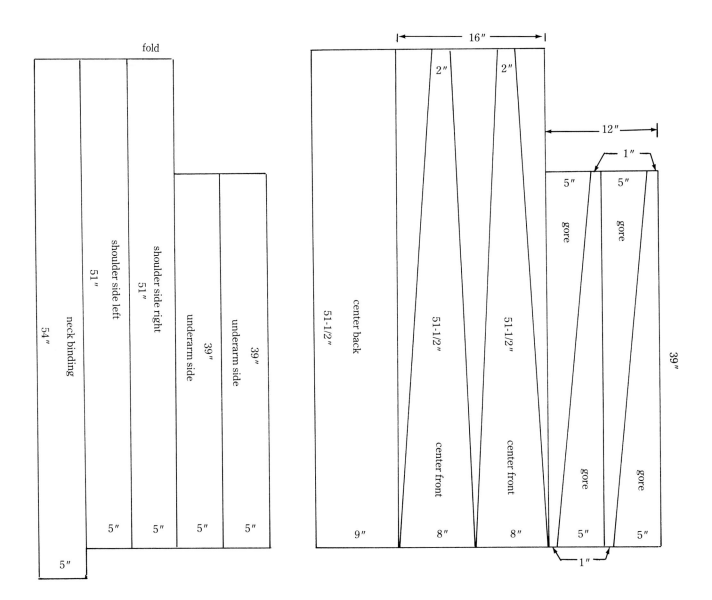

dimensions of pattern pieces

DIMENSIONS OF PATTERN PIECES: this coat is reversible and all seams are covered with binding. Each pattern piece has an outside and lining side. The dimensions are for a loosely fitting coat and INCLUDE 1/4″ seam allowance. Neck band, shoulder side right and shoulder side left panels are very long and can be pieced or cut on fold of fabric. These panels are all 5″ wide. Neck band is 108″ long or 54″ on fold, shoulder side panels are 102″ long or 51″ on fold. Underarm side panels are 5″ wide and 39″ long. Center panel front is cut in two pieces with seam at shoulder. Center panel back is 9″ wide and 51-1/2″ long. Center panel front is pieced in one 16″ wide by 51-1/2″ long panel and cut into two triangle shapes each 2″ at top and 8″ at bottom. See drawing for cutting diagram. Four gores (long triangles) for sides are also cut from one panel after piecing. Panel is 12″ wide by 39″ long. Gores are cut 1″ at top and 5″ at bottom. Cut as diagramed. Each gore has a straight side and an angled side. When sewing gores to underarm panel straight side of gore is sewn to underarm side panel. Angle side is sewn to shoulder side panel.

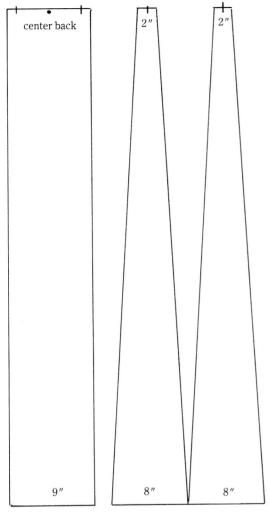

center panel back and fronts

TO CUT OUT COAT begin with the center panel. This can be pieced and lined before cutting out remainder of coat. In the sample coat all the triangle pieces were cut and pieced along with the center panel. Then the 5″ wide panels were cut, lined and hand quilted before assembling.

Sew 2″ edge of center panel front to center panel back matching outside edges. Match marks as shown. Stay stitch corners of neck opening and clip to corners. (See detail in Haori pattern.)

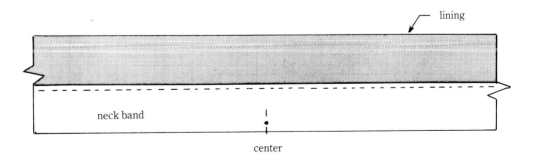

NECK BAND is 108″ long by 5″ wide. Cut matching lining and interface. With right sides together sew along one edge, turn and press seam. Mark center of neck band and match with center of neck opening. Sew neck band to neck opening with right sides together. Press seam and turn lining to inside and hand hem over seam.

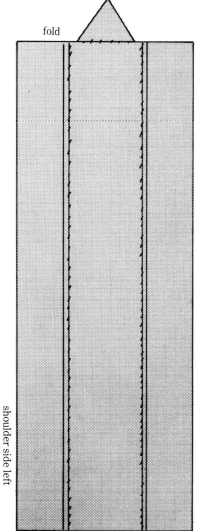

JOIN CENTER PANEL to shoulder side left and shoulder side right. Shoulder panels are 102″ long by 5″ wide. Cut lining to match. Sew shoulder panels to center front in one continuous seam from front hem over shoulder to back hem. Place binding over seam and stitch. Hand hem binding to lining.

join center panel

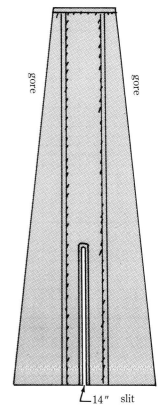

underarm unit

JOIN UNDERARM side panels to gores. Cut underarm panels 5″ wide by 39″ long. Cut lining. Cut gores 1″ at top and 5″ at bottom, 39″ long. Cut lining. Sew gores to each side of underarm panels with binding over seam. Each gore has a straight side and an angled side. When sewing gores to underarm panel straight side of gore is sewn to underarm side panel. Bind top edge of underarm side unit. Repeat for other side.

NOW: cut 14″ slit from hem edge directly in vertical center of underarm side panel. Sew binding around slit with 1/4″ seams. Hand hem binding to inside lining.

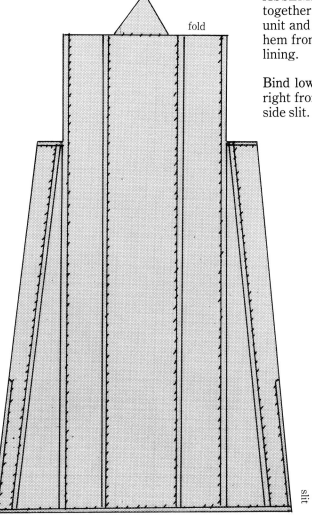

assemble coat

ASSEMBLE COAT by sewing side units to center panel. Pin right sides together with binding over the seam. Match lower hem edges of side unit and center panel. Sew from lower hem back over shoulder to lower hem front. This seam will finish the armhole edge. Hand hem binding to lining.

Bind lower hem of coat. This will take three pieces of binding; one for right front hem to side slit, one for back of coat, one for left front hem to side slit.

APPLIQUE shoulders with decorative fabric to stiffen so the shoulders will stand away from the body. Sholder panel is cut, lined and hem edges turned in and then the panel is appliqued to coat. Include seam allowances before cutting panel.

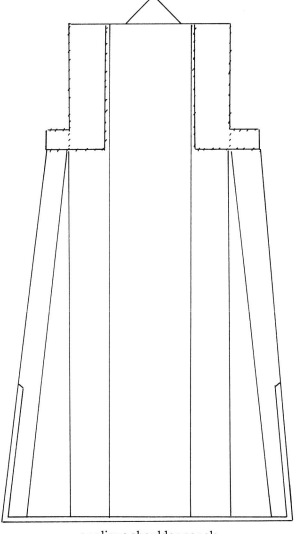

applique shoulder panels

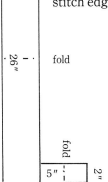

Shoulder panel is two pieces. One long piece finished 26" long by 4" wide or 13" on the fold and a small narrow piece finished 2" wide by 5" long. Sew small piece to lower edge of panel. Pin panel to coat. Hand stitch edges to coat and around armhole.

shoulder panel detail

Tibetan Vest

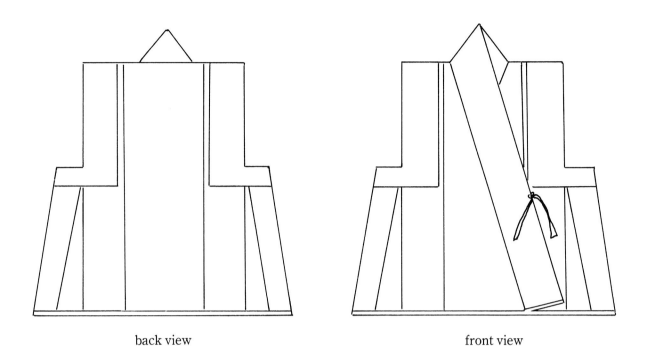

back view   front view

This is a short hip length version of the Tibetan sleeveless coat. The pattern is narrow panels alternating with gores (long triangles which add fullness). The center panel is wide and forms an exaggerated lifted shoulder which is trimmed with a stiffened fabric. The vest is loose fitting and is reversible. The front panel overlaps and is fastened with a self tie. The neck band is wide and folds down around the neck.

See color plate on page 46.

The original is a long sleeveless coat made in heavy wool fabric and the shoulders are trimmed with gold brocade.

TO DETERMINE FABRIC NEEDED: the sample vest was made in patchwork style from scraps left over from other projects. The long panels were cut from a piece of fabric at least as long as the panel itself. Measure from front hem over shoulder to back hem to determine length needed. In sample vest long panels measure 52" long. Vest can be made longer, shorter or panels can be made narrower for different sizes. All seams are finished with 1-1/2" wide straight grain binding sewn with 1/4" seam allowance and hand hemmed to inside lining.

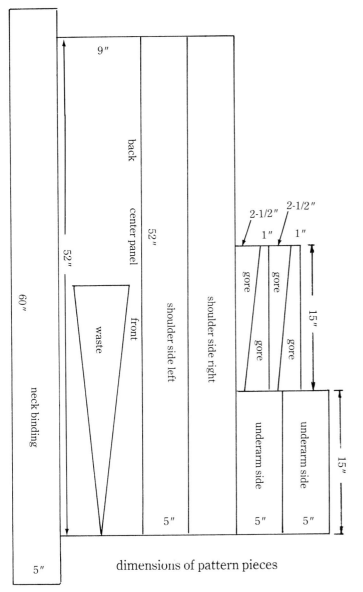

dimensions of pattern pieces

DIMENSIONS OF PATTERN PIECES: this vest is reversible and all seams are covered with binding. Each pattern piece has an outside and lining side. The seam allowance is 1/4″. Sew seams together with binding on top of seam, hand hem binding to lining. The dimensions are for medium size which fits loosely. Pattern pieces can be altered for larger or smaller vest. The dimensions given in the pattern INCLUDE the 1/4″ seam allowance.

Neck band is 60″ long by 5″ wide, cut two plus interfacing.

Center panel is 52″ long by 9″ wide.

Shoulder side right and shoulder side left panels are 52″ long by 5″ wide.

Underarm side panels are 15″ long by 5″ wide.

Gores at sides are 15″ long and 1″ at top and 2-1/2″ at bottom. Cut four gores. If using patchwork, piece gores as one flat piece and cut shapes as directed.

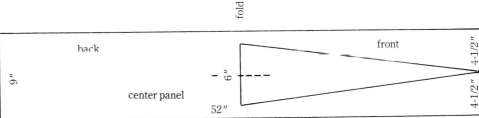

TO CUT OUT GARMENT begin with center panel which is cut 52″ long by 9″ wide. If using patchwork, piece center panel before cutting out center neck opening. Sample vest was pieced using large pieces of fabric in the string patchwork method, that is, cut an underlining to size of panel and sew pieces to underlining. Cut lining and pin to patchwork panel with wrong sides together. Handle as one layer.

Fold center panel in half matching hem edges and mark fold line. Open out panel and mark 6″ neck opening in middle of panel. Find center of panel at lower edge. Draw line from 6″ mark to center mark on hem. Cut out neck and center panel front opening. Stay stitch corners of neck opening and clip. (See detail in Haori pattern.)

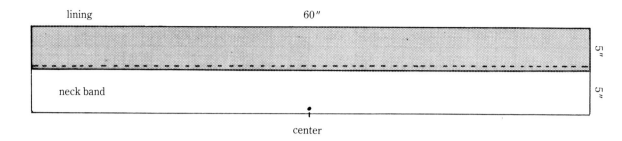

lining   60″

neck band

center

CUT OUT NECK BAND and lining 60″ long by 5″ wide. Interface neck band and sew band and lining together. With right sides together sew along one edge, turn and press. Mark center of neck band and match with center of neck opening. Stitch neck band to neck opening right sides together. Press seam and hand hem lining to inside.

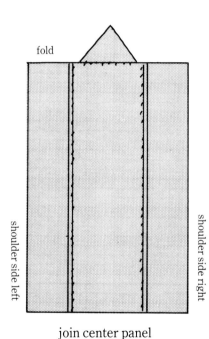

join center panel

JOIN CENTER PANEL to shoulder side left and shoulder side right. Panels are 52″ long by 5″ wide. Line and sew panels to center front panel with one continuous seam from front hem over shoulder to back hem. Place binding over seam and stitch. Hand hem binding to lining.

UNDERARM SIDE PANELS are cut 15″ long by 5″ wide and lined. Gores are pieced in one piece of fabric and then cut as diagramed. Line gores and sew to sides of underarm panel right sides together with binding over seam. Hand hem binding to inside. Each gore has a straight side and an angled side. When sewing gores to underarm panel straight side of gore is sewn to underarm side panel. Angle cut side is sewn to shoulder side panels.

Finish top edge of unit with binding and hem binding to inside.

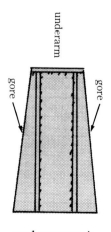

underarm unit

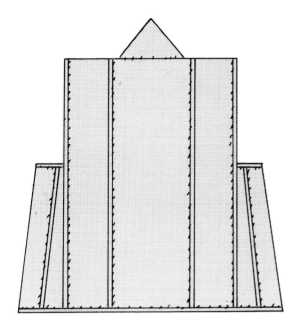

assemble vest

ASSEMBLE VEST by sewing side units to center panel unit with right sides together and binding over seam. Match lower hem edges and sew from lower hem over shoulder to lower hem. Hand hem binding to lining. This binding finishes the armhole edge.

Bind lower hem of vest.

APPLIQUE shoulders with decorative fabric to stiffen. Shoulders will stand away from the body. A lightweight fabric can be used but should be stiffened with underlining. Shoulder panel is cut, lined and hem edges turned in and then panel is hand appliqued to vest. Include seam allowance before cutting out panel.

Shoulder panel is two pieces. One long piece finished 26″ long by 4″ wide or 13″ on the fold and a small narrow piece finished 2″ wide by 5″ long. Sew small piece to lower edge of long panel. Pin panel to vest. Hand stitch edges to vest and around armhole edge.

Add a self tie if desired.

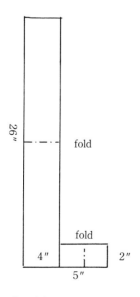

shoulder panel detail

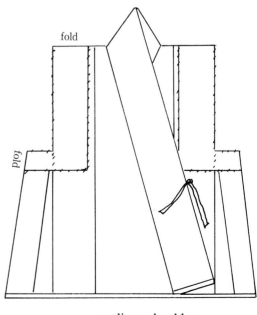

applique shoulders

G

G. Nine Patch Tunic
 Appliqued diamonds and nine patch
 gussets.

 Pattern on page 51.

H. Tibetan Vest
 String patchwork in large pieces,
 handquilted.

 Pattern on page 42.

I. Quilted Vest
 String patchwork with Seminole.

 Pattern on page 22.

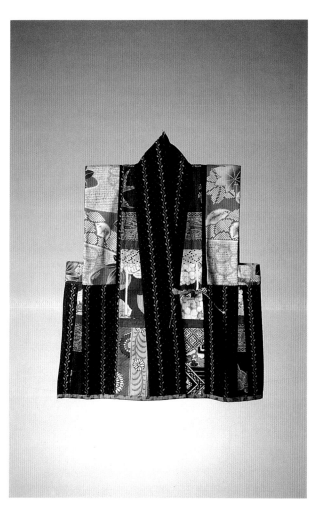

H

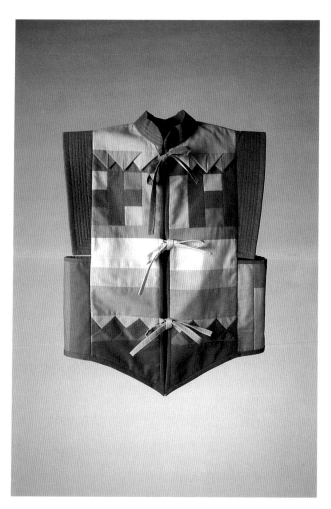

I

J

J. African Shirt
Strips of cotton machine pieced, lined, hand quilted.

Pattern on page 48.

K. African Cape
Silk crepe, china silk applique, silk brocade trim.

Pattern on page 49.

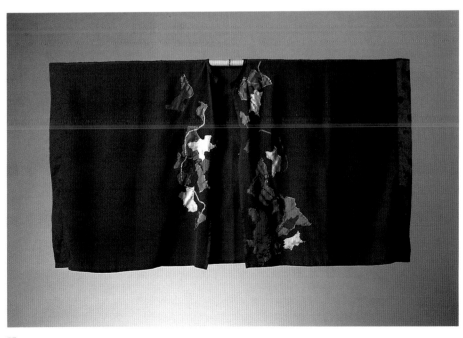

K

African Shirt

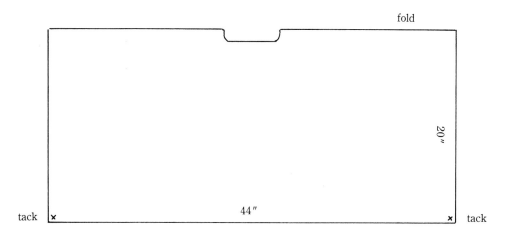

This rectangle becomes a very loose fitting pants top. The side seam is not sewn. The lower corners are tacked to fasten at hem.

The original shirt was designed to be cool in a very warm climate. It is lightweight cotton with embroidery around the neck opening.

TO DETERMINE FABRIC NEEDED: one size fits all and on the fold is 20″ long from shoulder to hem and 44″ wide. When opened out the top measures 40″ by 44″ plus hem allowance. 1-1/4 yards of 45″ fabric is adequate. The shirt can be made longer. If done in patchwork piece fabrics before cutting out shirt. Shirt is lined.

In the sample shirt strips of fabric were machine pieced and pressed. The pieced fabric was placed wrong sides together over a thin cotton lining. The two fabrics were handled as one for neck opening and hemming.

See color plate on page 47.

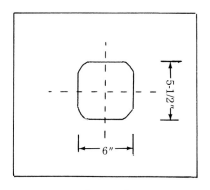

neck opening

NECK OPENING is a modified square directly in the middle of the 40″ by 44″ rectangle. The shirt is designed to wear either side front to back so neck opening is equal on both sides.

Neck opening is 6″ across and 5-1/2″ down. The corners are rounded off. Cut a facing out of fabric and center it on rectangle. Mark center vertical and horizontal lines on facing. Draw neck opening on facing. Stitch on drawn line. Cut out center leaving 1/4″ seam allowance. Clip curve and turn facing to inside. Press. Slip stitch facing to inside of shirt.

Hem sleeves and lower edge with narrow hem or cut 1-1/2″ straight grain binding and hem raw edges with 1/4″ seam allowance. Slip stitch binding to inside. Tack lower corners of side seams or attach narrow ties as in sample shirt.

WHEN CUTTING OUT GARMENT ALLOW SEAM ALLOWANCE ON ALL PIECES

African Cape

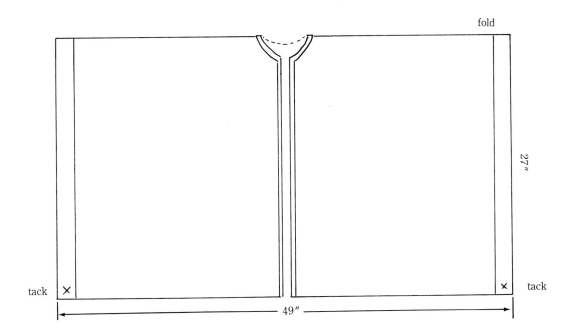

This is a variation of the African shirt pattern made into a cape. The cape has an opening in the center front with a round neck opening and is longer and wider than the shirt.

See color plate on page 47.

TO DETERMINE FABRIC NEEDED: one size fits all and on the fold measures 27" from shoulder to hem and 49" wide. The width measurement includes a 1-3/4" wide contrasting fabric binding on each sleeve edge. When opened out the rectangle measures 54" by 49" long.

In the sample cape silk crepe was used and china silk appliqued to the surface. Silk brocade was used as binding.

NECK OPENING is the round template from the back of this book. Mark the center vertical and horizontal on the rectangle and draw the template on the fabric. Slash the front opening to the lower edge. Bind the front opening with 1-1/2" wide straight grain binding sewn with 1/4" seam. Then bind the neck opening with 1-1/2" wide bias binding and 1/4" seam. Slip stitch bindings to inside. The neck binding covers the raw edge at the top of the front binding.

Decorate cape as desired. Add 1-3/4" wide binding to both sleeve edges. Cut binding 3-1/2" wide plus seam allowance and sew to sleeve edges. Slip stitch to inside.

Hem lower edge by hand or sew with binding.

Tack lower corners of side seams.

WHEN CUTTING OUT GARMENT ALLOW SEAM ALLOWANCE ON ALL PIECES

Tabbard

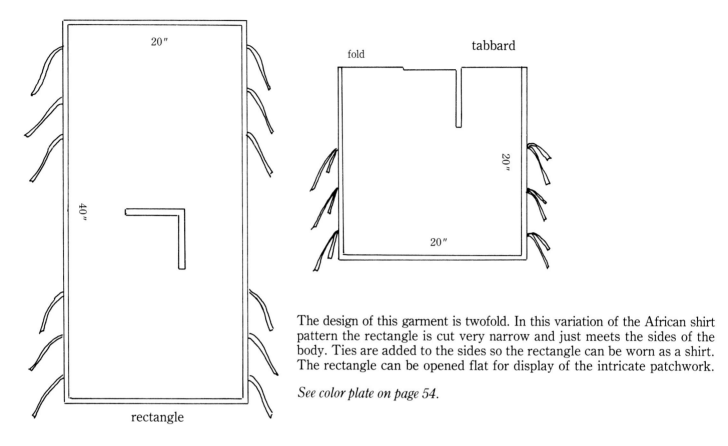

rectangle

tabbard

fold

The design of this garment is twofold. In this variation of the African shirt pattern the rectangle is cut very narrow and just meets the sides of the body. Ties are added to the sides so the rectangle can be worn as a shirt. The rectangle can be opened flat for display of the intricate patchwork.

See color plate on page 54.

TO DETERMINE FABRIC NEEDED: measure with a tape measure the width necessary to cover the body. Medium size should be about 40″ including ease. Divide that in half to determine width for the rectangle. The length should be just below the waist, measuring from front over shoulder to back waist. Rectangle for medium size is finished 20″ wide by 40″ long.

The sample shirt was machine pieced using strips of cotton and variations of the pieced square. The whole panel was used as the area for design, taking care to consider the design when also folded in half. A lining was cut the same size as the rectangle.

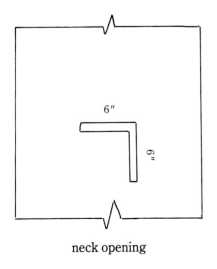

neck opening

NECK OPENING is very simple so not to obstruct the whole panel design. Place lining on pieced rectangle right sides together. Find center horizontal line and mark opening 6″ wide. At right edge of opening extend line 6″ vertically. Sew on both sides of drawn line and straight across ends. Clip between sewn lines and into corners. Turn and press.

Make narrow ties for sides.

Finish side edges with 1-1/2″ binding placing ties in seam. Slip stitch binding to inside.

Bind lower edge.

WHEN CUTTING OUT GARMENT ALLOW SEAM ALLOWANCE ON ALL PIECES

Nine Patch Tunic

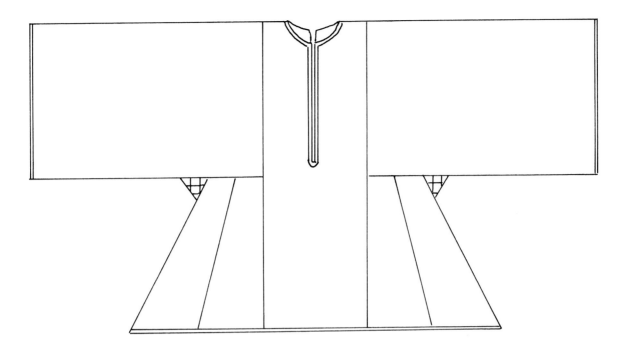

Very large loose fitting tunic has narrow center panel, large sleeves, multiple side panels. Underarm gussets are sewn in nine patch squares. Tunic is trimmed with narrow contrasting binding.

See color plate on page 46.

The original from Afghanistan is black cotton trimmed with 1/8″ wide binding and has embroidery on front skirt. The gussets are hand pieced silk nine patch squares.

TO DETERMINE FABRIC NEEDED: one size fits all. Center panel extends from front lower edge over shoulder to back hem 64″ long and 11″ wide. Sleeves are 25″ long and 16″ wide on the fold at shoulder or 32″ wide. Side panels are slightly shaped 3″ at top and 7″ at bottom. There are a total of 8 side panels. Two are on each side of center panel in front and back. Add seam allowance before cutting out panels, 1/4″ seams are adequate. Allow 2-1/2 yards for tunic plus 1/2 yard for narrow binding. Use scraps to piece nine patch gusset.

Sample tunic was sewn in black cotton with contrasting binding and has appliqued squares on the front.

WHEN CUTTING OUT GARMENT ALLOW SEAM ALLOWANCE ON ALL PIECES

DIMENSIONS OF PATTERN PIECES: center panel, sleeves, side panels as in diagram. Cut out center panel 11″ wide by 64″ long. Add seam allowance before cutting. Hem edge will be finished with contrasting binding.

dimensions of pattern pieces

NECK OPENING is from template in back of book. Mark center horizontal fold of center panel and trace neck opening directly on fabric. Slash front opening to 13″ and back center opening to 6″. Stay stitch on seam line around neck. Cut seam allowance away to 1/8″. Bind neck opening with bias binding with 1/8″ seam. Bind front and back opening with 1/8″ seam. Slip stitch binding to inside seam. Bar tack front slash opening at 5-1/2″ below neck opening. Fasten back neck opening with button or bar tack. Sample uses applique diamond as fastener.

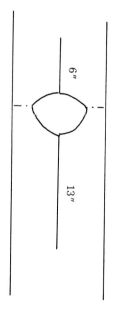

neck opening

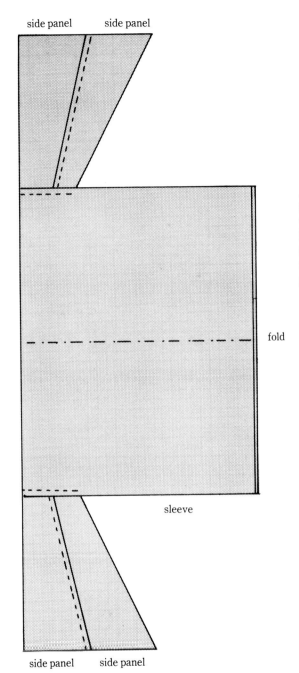

side panel   side panel

fold

sleeve

side panel   side panel

assemble sleeves and side panel

ASSEMBLE SLEEVES AND SIDE PANELS. Sleeves are 25" long by 32" wide plus seam allowance. Finish wrist edge of sleeve with 1/8" binding before assembling. Cut out side panels, a total of eight each measuring 3" at top and 7" at bottom and 16" long. See diagram for side panel shape. Sew two side panels together. Then sew top of side panels to sleeve underarm.

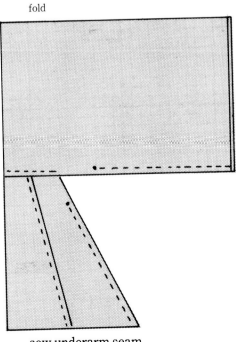

fold

sew underarm seam

SEW UNDERARM AND SIDE SEAMS to prepare for gusset. Sew sleeve from wrist edge with 1/4" seams leaving 3" open in seam for gusset. Sew side panel seam together leaving 3" open for gusset.

Pattern continues on page 56.

L

L. Wrap Around Skirt
Strips of fabric machine pieced, lined, hand quilted.

Pattern on page 57.

M. Tabbard
Folded to wear. Strips of cotton, variations of pieced square.

N

M

N. Tabbard
Open for display.

Pattern on page 50.

O

O. Tibetan Sleeveless Coat
  Night Rainbow. Silk and cotton string patchwork with some pieced squares. Handspun silk thread for quilted stitches. Handwoven fabric for shoulder panels.   *Pattern on page 37.*

Nine Patch Tunic continued.

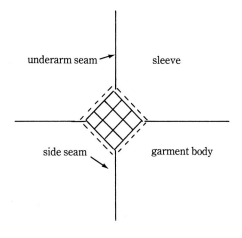

gusset

GUSSET is a nine patch square with 1″ by 1″ patches. Cut squares 1-1/2″ allowing for 1/4″ seams. Sew three patches together, join three rows of three patches. Sew gusset to underarm and side panel seams with 1/4″ seams. When completed, gusset forms triangle on the fold under the arm.

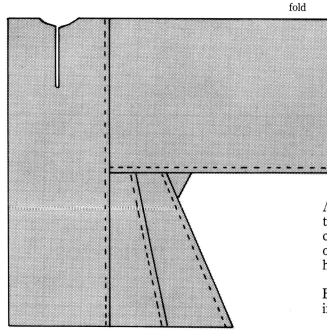

assemble tunic

ASSEMBLE TUNIC: mark shoulder fold line on center panel and sleeves. With right sides together stitch center panel to sleeve and side panels with one continuous seam from lower front hem over shoulder to back hem.

Bind lower edge of tunic. Decorate with applique if desired.

This pattern is very large but the pattern pieces can be made smaller for a closer fit.

56

Wrap Around Skirt

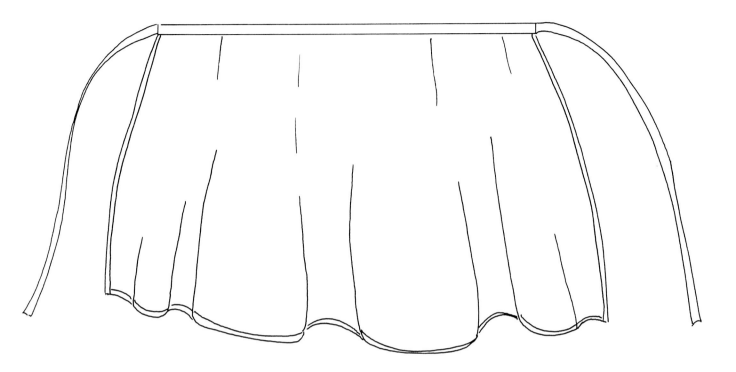

Slightly gathered rectangle sewn to a waistband has long ties which wrap around to tie in front.

See color plate on page 54.

TO DETERMINE FABRIC NEEDED: approximately 2 yards of fabric is needed for skirt. Measure from waist to hem for length. Waistband measurement is waist plus 12″ for wrap around band. To that measurement add 1/3 more to determine width for fullness of skirt.

TO SEW SKIRT cut out rectangle for skirt and piece or hand quilt to personal taste. Line skirt and gather at top.

Waistband is 1″ wide finished. Two 40″ long ties are finished to 1″ width and are sewn in ends of waistband. Cut two ties and waistband plus seam allowance.

Bind side edges of skirt panel to finish raw edges. Sew skirt to waistband, insert ties in waistband. Bind lower edge of skirt or hem.

ALLOW SEAM ALLOWANCE ON ALL PIECES BEFORE CUTTING OUT SKIRT.

Template

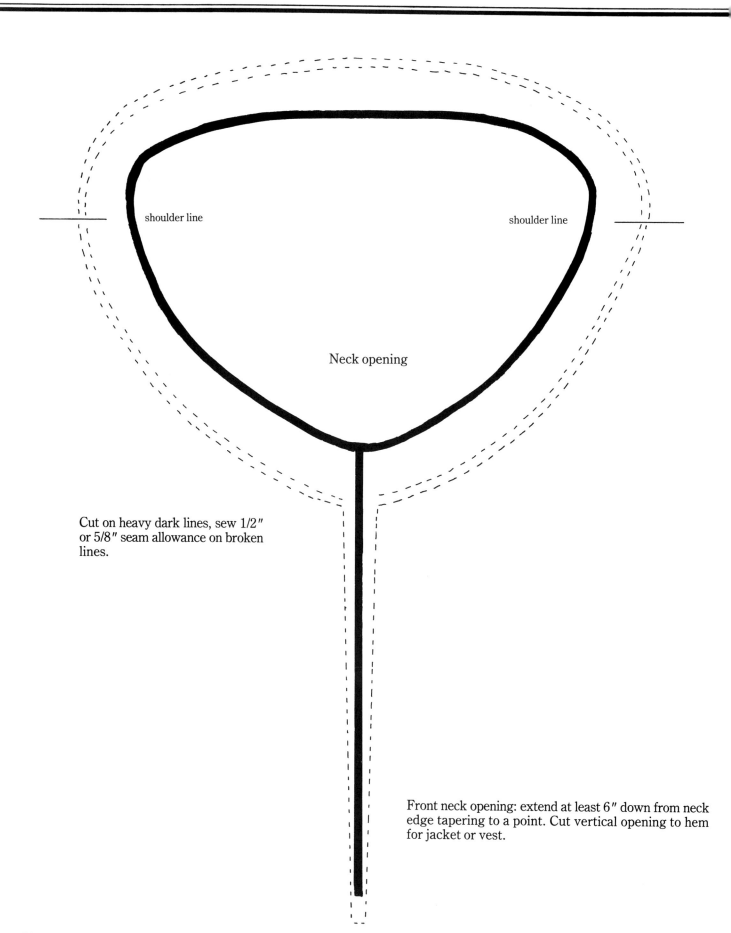

shoulder line

shoulder line

Neck opening

Cut on heavy dark lines, sew 1/2″ or 5/8″ seam allowance on broken lines.

Front neck opening: extend at least 6″ down from neck edge tapering to a point. Cut vertical opening to hem for jacket or vest.

Notes

Other Fine Quilting Books From C&T Publishing

For more information write for a free catalog from
C&T Publishing
P.O. Box 1456
Lafayette, CA 94549
(1-800-284-1114)